Passive Income

5 Proven Methods & Mindsets to Make 500-10000 a months in 45 days

Harvey Kinder

Table of Contents

INTRODUCTION

Year after year the cost of living and prices of everything you can put your hands on is escalating to new heights. However, it is an unfortunate fact that our incomes are not growing in the same way. With such heavy inflation, a large number of people need to take up multiple jobs in order to save money for the future. In fact, some people need to take on 2 to 3 jobs just to survive.

In a 24 hour day, if a person takes up 3 jobs, he will have absolutely no time for himself and his personal life. His family members will be neglected, he will be sleep deprived, mentally, physically and emotionally exhausted and extremely frustrated.

Taking up multiple jobs will bring in more income, but at what cost? Is it really worth exhausting yourself for a few extra bucks? Is it worth breaking your back and losing your sleep just to bring in that additional income? I'm sure you have heard the famous quote, "Health is wealth" and if you're going to sacrifice your health to make money, you're eventually going to have to sacrifice your money to regain your health.

Although such commitment and dedication are highly commendable, it isn't exactly feasible. It is necessary that you find alternative ways to rake in the big bucks. You need to figure out a way in which you can set up and build your very own business that will eventually bring you the income you have always desired.

Think of all those who have achieved utter and complete success in their lives. Think of those people who have left their mark in history purely due to their success. Try and imagine what it is that they did differently that made them a cut above the rest. What kind of an attitude and mindset did they sport that gave them the power to become successful. The answer is fairly straight and obvious. With the exception of those who were born with a silver spoon, the self-made successes were always proactive and didn't have the word lazy in their dictionaries. They had their heads screwed on right and most importantly knew and understood their priorities. They redirected their energies to the right path and made their businesses work for them and not the other way around. They discovered a way to make money on their own rather than being dependent on the money they brought in from dead-end jobs.

If you are wondering how to earn larger amounts of money without having to work for it, it's very simple. There's an economic term known as passive income and such income is generated without the need of having to invest extra hours on the job. This may not be the typical quit-your-job-and-get-rich-instantly kind of situation, If you want a silver bullet or super-easy way to earn $5,000/day clicking red buttons scammy stuff, This isn't for you.

Passive income simply means an income received on a regular basis, with little effort required to maintain it. To put it in layman's terms, passive income means you make your money, assets and resources work for you. It is a simple method that will require less work but will give you great returns.

At first setting up a successful source of passive income may require a lot of work and may also be time-consuming, however once established the rewards will most certainly pay off. Freedom, independence and an all but full control of your own time are some of the perks of this kind of business venture. Granted, the first steps towards your passive income system will require work, sometimes even hard work, but the end goal makes it all worthwhile. One way of looking at it would be this: within a year's time, with consistent effort, you may be well on your road to both freedom and security. Needless to mention, many people work an entire lifetime towards this goal, only to achieve it at old age.

Well, passive income is a lot like some initial hard word to begin with, but with the aim of having more time to relax later.

So are you ready? If you are, let's begin.

Chapter 1

Staring A Passive Income Business From Home: The Facts

If you've decided to start a small business, you've had enough of the bullshit that an unproductive 9 to 5 corporate job has to offer, you've come to a few conclusions about what it will be like to be your own boss, set your own hours, and work from home (or anywhere with an bloody Internet connection). The pull to generate income while still dressed in your pajamas may be strong, but it shouldn't be the only motivation behind a new business venture.

The truth is there are many things to consider when starting up a home-based business. We'll expand on five unique opportunities that are easy to start from home and don't makeup to big, fat hole in your pocket, but first you must decide if you are up to the challenge.

Ask yourself these questions

1. What things am I passionate about? What areas am I talented in?
2. How much time can I afford to invest in a new business?
3. What resources do I already have?
4. How much am I willing to invest?
5. What is an approximate, allowable time frame to get a business up and running?

We'll discuss these questions and more in the following pages, but they are a great place to start when considering an affordable, home-based business venture. Be specific with your answers here, and as you read through the five unique opportunities, ask yourself which one would fit best according to the answers you have given.

Working from home takes self-motivation, understanding of your market, and diligence. It does take hard work and perseverance, but the benefits far outweigh the effort. You will be your own boss, be responsible for your schedule, and have the opportunity to make important business decisions based on what is best for *you*.

Starting a Passive income stream will be the most rewarding thing you can do.

Where to start

After you have thoughtfully gone over the questions from the previous section, take a moment to brainstorm and dream. Use paper or a whiteboard to write out your ideas. Don't limit yourself to things you've done in the past, but embrace new ideas. Write out all ideas, even if you don't think they are possible at this point.

Take a half an hour or so to expand upon the first question, "What things am I passionate about? What areas am I talented in?" Be general as well as specific, listing out known jobs that are associated with your passions as well as the things you possess talent in. This is more than creating a resume; it's compiling a list of things that will add to your energy level on a daily basis.

When you've done this, type them up into a document and save them in a folder on your computer. This will be a great resource to keep. Once your business is up and running, this document can be something you refer back to for new ideas and ways to expand.

Why Passion and Talent Go Hand in Hand

In this eBook we'll discuss selling on eBay, creating an Etsy store, opening an online bookstore, freelance writing, and independent coaching, but these aren't the only options for starting a home-based business. In some ways, the possibilities are endless. At this stage of the process though, discovering what you are passionate about *and* what you are talented in is crucial for several reasons.

Passion

Evaluating the areas where you are passionate allows you to understand yourself and your desires better. Doing passionate things comes naturally to us. We allocate our time to them and are less likely to find the tasks boring or uninspiring if they are within the realm of our passions.

One of the main reasons that we feel discouraged or unenergetic at work can be due to the fact that we are operating outside of our passions. When you are required to complete a task at work that uses none of your passions, that task becomes harder and there is less motivation to accomplish it. These actions take more energy from us and create additional stress. No one likes to work in those conditions.

Talent

When completing the brainstorming exercise, take into account the things you already know you excel at. These things are your talents. They don't all stem from work related things, but they can deal with your past experience and job knowledge.

It's important to recognize that there may be things that you are passionate about, but are not equally talented in. The result of choosing a job that capitalizes on passions without the preparation of talent creates stress and confusion. You will constantly feel inadequate, underprepared, and self-conscious.

The best job for any individual is one that seamlessly combines their passions and their talents.

During the initial start up phase, you may discover a job idea that isn't expanded upon here, but the information contained in these pages will still be helpful to you. Much of what we will discuss for each job has far reaching implications to many online businesses.

When you have completed your time of brainstorming, understand the things you are passionate about, and have taken into account your talents, take a step away from thinking about this new business venture. It's easy to become so excited you obsess over the idea itself instead of the logical process to starting up a business.

For the rest of this eBook we will look at the best ways to start a new business from home that won't be expensive to begin, but will combine your passions and talents into a money making endeavor.

Chapter 2

The 6-Figure Business Mindset

Running a Business is a rewarding and exciting venture. You will likely face difficulties, but you will also reap rewards and benefits.

Always keep in mind that the ability to create is not something that just happens without work though. You can't just sit down with a paper and pen and expect an idea to just appear. Well okay, this does happen for some people, like Mark Zuckerberg creating Facebook, but even this took planning and a no small amount of work. You want to try to find a niche that works well for you. You want to find a business idea that suits your strengths.

To prepare to break into the niche field that you have selected you should start with research. There are quite a few resources you can use for your research. You should study blogs as they can give you a great deal of insight into what different people are doing in your area business. Also listen to podcasts, as they will contain a good amount of information from interviews with other self-employed individuals, and they can be uplifting, or inspiring to hear the success stories of others.

Search Engines results will give you a great way to find new information about your business, and the product or service that you want to offer. The search engine results will also direct you to emerging competition, and additional research that you may need to break into your niche. You can also read, there are a variety of books that will help you in your chosen business area.

We've compiled a list of additional things to consider when starting a Business.

Branding

We've mentioned branding a few times throughout the pages of this book, but it's worth another mention. Branding for your business is very important, no matter what business you decide to start. The extent you go to in order to brand yourself may look different depending on your budget, but these are some initial questions to ask:

- *What is the main idea of my business?*
  This is your vision statement and should affect every decision you make with reference to your business.

- *What makes me different than others in this business?*
  This is your selling point. Why would someone choose you or your business over someone else that is doing/selling the same thing?

- *Who am I selling to?*
  This is your audience and you *must* know who they are, what they like, and what is important to them.

Start with these questions and, as your business grows, reevaluate them as needed.

Marketing

A large part of home-based business success is dependent on your discoverability as an individual or company. The ideas put forth in this eBook won't be difficult to implement and will have you up and running almost immediately, but the long-term perspective must also be part of the startup stages of your business.

Remember:

- Take time to build a responsive audience through social media.
- Spend money to market yourself *only* when you can see direct results to that marketing.
- Use your vision and speak directly to your audience through all forms of marketing.

Sellers Community

No matter what Business venture you head into, you will automatically find yourself in a seller's community. Some of these communities are stronger or more vibrant than others. Etsy is a good example of a very strong selling community.

We recommend that you discover what that community is and take part in joining it. This may also look like areas where community members congregate, like forums, online chat rooms, or even email chains. Discover what the community looks like for your Business.

Goals

We have discussed short-term and long-term goals, but here is where they are put into practice. Once you've deiced on the type of business you are going to start and you've created your business plan, it's time to put your goals into affect. You may need to hone the goals into accomplishable sections (don't take on too much at once) and then work toward each goal, one at a time.

After the first six months of being in business, sit down and reevaluate your goals. Do this again at the first year mark. After that, you may be able to stretch out your goal sessions to once a year, but always be pushing yourself forward. Think of new ways to improve your business, expand your reach, and increase your sales. If necessary, ask for help.

Staying in Business

As time progresses, you may find yourself facing the question of whether or not you should stay in business. The main thing when making this assessment is passion.

Are you still passionate about what you are doing?

Remember that brainstorming exercise we did? Now is the time to remember what you were passionate about in the beginning. When you start up your business, base your decision on your passion in line with your talents and know that hard work will be a requirement, but it will also be a labor of love. Doing what you are passionate about will make that hard work worth it in the end.

If at any point in your business the hard word becomes overwhelming, it's time to take a step back and reevaluate. Go back and ask yourself the questions about why you wanted to start a Business in the first place. Talk to others (either in person or via email) who are in your line of work and gain inspiration from them. Lastly, remember your passion. Your Business with thrive when it is based on that passion and you must always keep that before you.

Chapter 3

Selling On eBay: An Untapped Resource

The average Internet search will land you millions of possibilities to purchase items from all over the world. We often turn to a company website or Amazon for reliable options, but right there, alongside most search engine results, it's not uncommon to find an eBay option for an item you're looking for.

These options tend to represent name brand clothing, electronics, and technology, but did you know that there are categories for purchasing cars, sports equipment, toys, gardening items, and even art and collectables? These, along with many other items you wouldn't think to find on eBay, are a wealth of untapped resources to the discerning, entrepreneurs' eye.

Starting a business on eBay is one of the most popular ways to go into business simply because you can be as casual or as serious about it as you like. For someone with high demands on their time, it's an ideal business venture because a few hours spent researching and posting items starts the ball rolling for the rest of the week.

For the serious eBay seller, there is a higher level of dedication required to truly capitalize on the eBay selling culture. This dedication requires planning, forethought to purchases, and often trips to thrift stores or estate auctions. The commitment to search for popular, saleable items doesn't come without rewards though. The proper forethought will earn you higher returns for the additional effort. In addition to these things, you will also spend time researching before and after so that your prices can be competitive as well as appropriate.

Let's take a look at the numerous benefits to starting a Business as an eBay seller.

Three T's of Selling on EBay

Time

There are many things to consider when deciding to start a business from home. Paramount to everything else is the time and effort you will be dedicating to this business. As previously mentioned, eBay is a great option for anyone no matter the amount of time they can spend listing items. However, to be successful enough to replace a full-time job, you will need to be willing to expend time and energy toward your eBay business. This time won't be wasted, but will significantly affect your return.

Consider these elements that will require you time:

Setting up and maintaining an active profile in good standing on eBay:
Though not an extensive process, your eBay profile will require maintenance. Initially, it may take upwards of twenty minutes to set up your profile with all of the correct information. Following this initial setup period, much less time will be required, though you will want to maintain good response times for any

questions (customer service), leave feedback for all sales and purchases made, and keeping your information up to date as needed.

Finding items to list: Depending on the level of involvement you wish to have with your eBay business, you will need to budget your time accordingly when it comes to finding items to sell. For most, this initially looks like cleaning out closets and going through your garage for saleable items. As time progresses, and your business grows, you will want to adjust your time expectations to include trips to local thrift stores, antique road shows, estate sales, and auctions. This time will also include online research for items that may be listed for upcoming auctions or for something you place on hold at a thrift store. Online research is fascinating, but it will take time.

Listing items: Once you've spent the time collecting your sale items, no matter their origin, you will need to prepare them for listing. This will include taking photos, writing up descriptions, and finding the appropriate price for sale (whether initial auction price or buy now option).

Shipping sold items: After your items have sold, you will then be responsible for packaging them and then shipping them. This isn't necessarily time consuming, but you will need to factor in your proposed shipping time period (typically 3-5 business days) as well as time spent at the post office. This will vary depending on day of the week and season.

Type

Before you begin your eBay Business, we recommend you consider what type of eBay seller you will be. Is this a casual business you will attend to on weekends or after work, here and there? Is this a business you are hoping to jump into in full force? Or, is this a business that you will start small with the desire to grow into something larger?

Each of these options is easily accomplished, but it will help for you to have goals in mind. Just as any business assesses their business plan before beginning, you can start your eBay Business with a plan in mind.

Ask these questions:

1. What are my short-term (6 month) goals?
2. Where do I want my business to be a year from now?
3. What are my long-term goals (3, 5, and 10 years)?

These questions may appear a bit extreme, but if you plan out where you are headed before you begin, it is more likely you will succeed.

Tasks

The last "T" of selling on eBay is "tasks". What we mean by this is taking into account the full understanding of tasks involved. We'll go over this in greater detail in the *Step by Step* portion below, but you must understand the tasks involved with selling on eBay.

Just as you must account for time to complete these tasks, the tasks themselves are equally important. As previously mentioned, customer service is a very important task for your eBay business. You must have the ability to reply to comments and feedback as quickly as possible in order to establish an excellent rating on eBay as a seller and a purchaser.

The Benefits

Selling on eBay comes with many benefits most jobs will not afford you. As you consider setting up a Business as an eBay seller, think over these benefits to opening your own account.

- Easy and Quick Setup

It is a simple and quick process to become a seller on eBay. It hardly takes any time to create a profile, upload a photo, and fill in basic information. We'll outline the steps below, but eBay has made it almost too easy to become a seller. For a Business owner, this is a definite plus!

- Work Remotely

Feel like working from Starbucks? Go right ahead. One of the best parts about starting a business selling on eBay is that you can work anywhere that has a strong wireless connection. This opens up myriad possibilities, but will also save you money when considering office space and/or Internet usage. Your office is anywhere you and your computer are. If you decided to take an extended vacation, you only require an Internet connection to check in on your items.

In addition to this, depending on your selling schedule and time frame, you can use your smart phone for everything from listing items to leaving feedback. The only requirement for you is in regards to shipping in a timely manner.

- Be your own boss

When most people consider starting their own business, a lot of thought goes into the pros and cons. A pro to working independently is the fact that you can be your own boss. You work on *your* time schedule, not someone else's. For those that possess qualities of self-starting and motivation, this is an excellent reason to start up an eBay business.

- Sell in your area of expertise

Another noted benefit of having your own eBay business is the fact that you can work in your area of expertise, in your passion. Since eBay is so multifaceted, you can capitalize on selling in areas where you have a marked interest or expanded knowledge. For example, if you possess knowledge about antique baseball paraphernalia, you can choose to hone your eBay profile to that area, branching out when you have the time and resources to sell additional items.

The Drawbacks

Though there are many benefits to starting up a business on eBay, there are a few downsides. Most of these drawbacks come into play when considering eBay as a full-time endeavor. Though they are notable, you must consider if they are significant enough to affect you at the start-up stages of your business.

- Demanding Customers

The portion of eBay that is made up of independent sellers is heavily reliant on customer feedback. The importance of service ratings on eBay elevate customer service to an extremely high position within the perspective of the sellers account itself. Customers are more likely to purchase from you should you have a higher ratings and positive feedback.

Unfortunately, there is no control over someone's feedback. The response that is given will be based on the item you've supplied, accuracy in description, the purchaser's interactions with you, and their overall satisfaction. You cannot control someone's experience with you, though you can go above and beyond to supply him or her with excellent customer service.

As with any business, the customer must have an elevated status in your mind as the business owner. This can be difficult when you deal with demanding customers, but is a natural part of running a business.

- No Absolutes on Prices

You may have done excellent research and feel confident in the price of the product you are putting forward, but the buyer may not always agree. This may look like lower bids or uninterested parties should your prices be too high. This will not be a problem in some cases due to the fact that, by slightly lowering the price, you can sell the item. This becomes increasingly problematic when a price threatens to dip below the amount you purchased it for or the item itself does not sell as you'd hoped.

There are no guarantees when selling on eBay. You must be diligent to research the market you will be selling in, price your items competitively, and be willing to lower some prices in order to move your inventory (unless you can afford the time and space to let the item sit until it is once again in demand).

- Fees

Likely the most apparent drawback to selling on eBay is the many fees involved with selling through their platform. These fees will differ depending on the items you sell. There can be fees associated with listing items, fees on your total sale amount, fees associated with the payment system you use (PayPal is one such vehicle) and other additional fees outlined on the eBay website. Unfortunately, these fees change often and will take a cut from your overall sale. There is no way around them.

The best advice to dealing with the drawback of fees is to take into account the price of the item you purchased, the price you wish to sell it for, and then subtract the fee from that price. If the total reached is not an allowable return on your investment, you should reconsider your listing price.

Step by Step: What it takes to set up a successful eBay store

1. **Open your account**

Begin your journey to selling on eBay by opening an account, filling out the profile items, and uploading a photo.

2. Decide on a listing

Choose what you will sell, whether that's a name brand item you've grown tired of or an item from a thrift store that will sell for a higher price than what you purchased it for. Then you will need to fill in these things:

Item and description

Most of the time you will be able to find an item that is similar to what you are selling. Use that item and its description to make the listing process go faster. Include a bit of personality in your description and possibly a personal recommendation should it apply.

Make sure you change all of the details to accurately match your listed item.

Photos

You will then need to upload photos of the item. It is best to take as many images as possible that show off every feature of the item you are selling.

Make sure the quality is as good as possible. If listing a name brand item, capture the tag up close. If there is a defect, be sure to take a picture of it as well as note this in your description.

<u>Price</u>

There are two options for pricing on eBay: fixed and auction. For fixed pricing, you choose the price that the item can be bought at and then list the item. For auction pricing, you list the initial bid, and then allow the price to be driven up by bidding. You can also add an option for your customers to buy the item immediately but be careful of this. They may offer you a good price, but the question remains: is it the *best* price? Allow your listing to go almost the full length of time before accepting these offers if you believe the bidding may take the price above what was suggested.

Most of the time the best option for selling popular items is through auction.

<u>Duration of the sale and schedule</u>
You have the option of making the sale the length of 3, 5, 7, or 10 days long depending on your preference. You can then choose when the item will go live based on the scheduling option.

Most sales are best left at a week's time.

<u>Shipping</u>

Lastly, you will give the option of shipping details. You can choose a flat rate option, which makes the shipping the same no matter the buyer, a calculated option that will depend on the customer's location, or a local pickup, which would include no shipping.

It is recommended to list shipping as free as often as possible to draw potential customers. However, you may need to build this into your price.

After you've taken care of these items, you are ready to sell. Wasn't that easy?

3. Customer Service

The next part of your eBay business setup involves customer service. This is incredibly important and can, in some cases, make or break the sale. Often, customers will have questions about an item and will email you through eBay's messaging system. They may ask for clarification if your description left them with questions, measurements of something, or possibly about the shipping time frame should it be something they want quickly.

Answer these and any questions with understanding, patience, and an eye toward making the customer's experience the best possible. Your ratings will be your reward!

4. Ship it out

When the time runs out and your item is sold, your next step is to ship it out. The shipping options you provided will guide you in the best way to ship your items. For many items, labels can be generated directly from eBay itself. This is a handy and timesaving feature that eBay offers. The funds for the shipping will come directly from the sale itself and, as long as you have the proper shipping containers, you will be able to get the item in the mail without hassle.

USPS offers many Priority Mails, flat-rate boxes and envelopes to be shipped to you for free. Visit their website to sign up to receive them.

5. Leave Feedback

After your items have been shipped you will have the option of detailing your experience with the customer. Always leave accurate, helpful feedback as quickly as possible.

6. Get Your Paycheck

Once the items are marked as delivered to your customer, eBay will then release your funds to then be transferred into your account (typically PayPal) minus any fees incurred.

Due to the uncertain nature of the mail system at times, make sure to update your tracking number as proof of mailing and to cover all of your bases should something go "missing" during the shipping process.

What you need

We've compiled a simple list of suggested items that you will need in order to set up your Business as an eBay seller.

- Computer
- Email address
- Phone number
- PayPal Account (free)
- Camera (a phone will do)
- Items to sell

Spend Less

Ways to save money while starting your eBay business:

- Use your phone's camera to take listing photos
- List items you have on hand
- Use free promotion like Facebook, Twitter, and Pinterest to attract potential buyers to your sale page
- Vista print offers inexpensive business cards in large number that can easily be customized.

Spend More

These ideas may cost a little more and may be best put into effect later in your eBay-selling journey.

- A good quality camera and dedicated area to photo your items (a plain background with good light is recommended)
- A customized cover photo and headshot image of high quality that highlights your business name and potentially features a theme in line with what you sell.
- High quality, customized cards and/or notes for your customers. These little notes can direct your clients back to your eBay store through colorful and creative images and a description of what you typically list.

Chapter 4

ETSY Store: 3 Steps To Turn Your Creativity Into Profit

Etsy is like a gold mine for those who are gifted with creative talent or have an affinity for art, design, crafts, or antiques. If you are talented and passionate in any of these areas, Etsy may just be the perfect place for you to begin your Business journey.

When considering an Etsy shop, there are many avenues you could take.

- Art
- Home Décor
- Handmade Jewelry
- Women and Men's clothing (modern and vintage)
- Children's clothing
- Handmade crafts
- Craft supplies
- Wedding accessories
- Graphic Designed elements (print and digital)
- Vintage items (classified as being over 20 years old)
- Consulting services

Some of these areas overlap which means there are nearly endless possibilities for creating an Etsy shop that is unique to you and your passions.

Now is the perfect time to consult your previous brainstorming list. Look through all of the passions as well as the talents that you have to decide on a focus for your shop. If you have the ability to craft, knit, or sew, you may consider starting up a handmade shop full of small, easily made items. Maybe your talents lie in graphic design? If so, you could create templates, cards, and logos for clients.

The possibilities are endless, but a word of advice here: When deciding on what to offer in your shop, consider your overall branding (we will also take a look at this under "Tips and Tricks for Small Businesses"). Shops that do the best and sell *most consistently* generally have an overall, established brand to their shop. This doesn't mean that you avoid including multiple selling items and options, but it does mean you should take time to decide what you will capitalize on.

Example: If you are fond of the country style, you may decide to give your shop country flair. This could look like a gingham pattern for your cover banner area and themed items that relate to your love of "all things country". This will be seen in the type of items you list, such as décor that has a shabby-chic feel to it.

This idea may seem slightly limiting, but consider this from a marketing standpoint. When your customers know what to expect from you, they are more likely to turn to your products because they can trust them. You will also have the ability to build a returning clientele based on the fact that they know what to expect from you. Consistency in product and in branding is essential to a successful business.

The Benefits

Selling on Etsy has many benefits. Some are similar to eBay but some differ as well.

- Freedom

The same freedom you will feel with eBay can be seen as an Etsy seller. It is, however, a different type of freedom. You are your own boss, able to establish you own hours as well as your own products, but there is the added constraint of creating the saleable product during a sufficient time period.

In some cases, the items you are selling are "made to order". In this case, you must be able to quickly produce the item (or note that there is an extended production time in the listing).

- Creativity

Unlike eBay, Etsy is all about *your* creativity. You are the designer *and* the businessperson and therefore in control of all aspects of your product. This is a liberating feeling and one that can make an Etsy career extremely rewarding for those who are creative.

- Broad Reach

The idea of Etsy is similar to that of an arts and crafts fair hosted online. The benefit to this is the fact that you do not need to pack up your items and travel.

You also have the added bonus of a much-extended reach. Your Etsy shop is a virtual store that can be open 24/7 around the globe should you want it to be. Your limitation is only on your ability to market your shop and to create products that sell.

The Drawbacks

- The business end

Etsy is geared toward those who have creative talent. Though it doesn't require that talent to open a store, it will be crucial you can provide that talent in order to sustain the store. Though this is not a rule, often people who are more gifted in creativity can struggle with the business end of owning and running a shop. This will only be a problem should you notice your own inabilities to a) sustain your creativity *and* your shop, b) find yourself failing at the business decisions and responsibilities needed to run the store, or c) feel overwhelmed running both aspects.

In the case of any of these options, you should seek out help from someone who has more knowledge of business. This is a great time to trade talents. Seek out someone willing to help you with things like accounting or marketing in exchange for a product you provide or your own creative perspective. If you can't find that type of deal, there is always the option to hire out. Likely, by the time you begin to feel the strain between business and creativity, you will be making sufficient funds to cover contracted help.

- Turnaround Time

As mentioned before, the turnaround time of supplying an item to a customer could become an issue. It is wise in this case to know exactly how long it will take you to create every item you list in your shop (should you decided not to keep them stocked). For some who are creative and rely on a "creative mood" to produce their product, this could prove to be a problem.

It is best to only list items in your shop that can be created, personalized, and shipped within a reasonable timeframe.

- Fees

Fees are almost always a concern when starting up an online business. Etsy includes a $0.20 fee for every item that is listed. They also have a transaction fee for each item that sells. As you would on eBay, take the time to map out the sale price minus the cost of production and fees to ensure you have accurately priced your item for the time, materials, and work that has gone into it.

Step by Step: What it takes to have a creative and successful shop on Etsy

Setting up shop on Etsy is as easy as 1—2—3!

1. **Set up your shop**

Pick a Username

This name is *not* the same as the shop name but is instead a name you will be identified with as the user on Etsy. You will not be able to change this name once you set it up.

Shop Name

This is the name of your shop. Again, put thought into what name you will use. This is a great time to consider the future plans of your business. Don't pick something that will limit you in the future. This name *can* be changed, but you don't want to confuse your potential clients either. Instead, pick a name that you can grow with.

Shop Policies

This part is very important. It is highly recommended that you write up your shop policies going over all of the main areas of commerce on Etsy including receiving payments, shipping charges, returns, exchanges, and refunds. Set this up in advance and be through so you will be covered should anything happen in the future.

Choose Payment Method

Set this portion up to give options for how you will receive payment.

<u>Add Items</u>

In your dashboard area there will be a "listings manager" that will be the area where you will list your items. Use this to list the items you wish to have displayed when you open your shop.

2. Open your Shop

And just like that, you're shop is ready to go! Choose to open your shop and start spreading the word. Marketing and sharing on social media will be a great way to draw attention to your shop. Use the widget option to add your shop to an existing blog (or if you start one) and be sure to share the good news with friends and family. Word of mouth is one of the *best* ways to draw customers.

3. Start selling

As you draw attention thorough your marketing efforts, you will start selling items. Make sure you are quick to ship the items out (finalizing them as quickly as possible) and answering any questions that may arise.

As with any business, customer service must be your top priority. Be a responsive and helpful shop owner, answering questions quickly and shipping items within your stated timeframe. You also can choose the option to offer "customized" items should you be ready and available to do so.

What you need

These items are recommended when starting your Etsy business:

- Computer
- Email address
- Phone number
- Shop name
- PayPal Account (free)
- Camera
- Supplies list of items you will create

Spend Less

To open your Etsy store quickly and for the least amount of startup cost consider these things:

- Use free photo programs to create a simple shop banner
- Decide on products (we recommend up to 5 different products) that can be quickly and easily made for a low cost.
- Start with smaller items. The cost in production and shipping will be lower.
- Don't create a lot of stock to begin with – this could end up as "wasted" money spent if that particular item does not sell.
- Consider soon-approaching holidays and decide what you can provide that fits in with that theme.
- Use Pinterest to pin items you sell.

- Start a blog (for free) and chronicle your processes to creating certain items in your shop

Spend More

To spend more on your shop, or as ideas of things to incorporate later in your shop, we recommend:

- Hire a graphic designer to create a customized shop banner that represents your specified theme. We would recommend using the same designer to make sure the images and style match on your social media sites as well as your blog template.
- Do market research on what items are selling well (based on your niche) and create products that rival these items but are uniquely yours. This may mean using higher quality materials and raising your prices.
- Purchase a good camera (or hire a local photographer) to take stunning product images. The quality of these images *will* make the difference in your shop.
- Diversify the products that you supply to reach a greater audience.
- Pay for advertising. (We recommend you keep track of how much you pay and what the *direct* results for this advertising are. You must evaluate if they are actually worth it.)

Chapter 5

Online Bookstore: A Booksellers Paradise

If you have a love for books and are considering starting up an online, Business, why not combine these two? An online bookstore can be the perfect outlet for someone interested in online business. There are many options for this, including varying degrees of startup costs and saleable stock. Below, we'll take a look at two very different approaches you can take to starting your own online bookstore, but first let's look at the benefits and drawbacks.

The Benefits

- Hobby to Business

If you are someone who loves reading and has a personal library already, then this is a great way to turn a hobby into a business. Opening an online bookstore can turn your love of books into a money-making venture.

- Online

Opening a brick and mortar bookstore may seem impossible at this point in your business journey, but an online store provides a lot of the same possibilities without the huge startup costs of a store.

- Financially Beneficial

What may potentially surprise you is that many first and second edition books and other, early titles are worth quite a bit of money. Should you have the time and resources to collect appropriate titles, you could potentially turn the sale of those items into a large payday.

- Global Reach

The love for books spans the globe. When opening an online bookstore, there is the possibility to have customers from all over the world (the only downside to this is international shipping).

The Drawbacks

- Dedication and Research

To open an online bookstore, you need to be willing to do your research. Whether you are pricing first edition novels or reselling college textbooks, you will need to ensure that your prices are competitive but also accurate in order to create a profit.

- Storage

Books take up a lot of room. We recommend that you have a decided space (either a room or garage space) to store your books. You must also consider the atmosphere of this space to ensure it is conducive to storing books (especially if they are rare and require special care).

- Shipping

Starting an online bookstore that deals with the sale of books means that frequent trips to the post office will be on your regular to-do list.

What you need

When considering an online bookstore, it is recommended you have these items to begin:

- Computer
- Online presence (a website)
- Bookselling platform: If not on your website, then via Amazon or other selling sites
- Books

Two Types of Online Bookstores

The first thing you'll need to do before taking any steps is deciding on what type of online bookstore you will be and what capital you can afford to put into the startup of your store.

Book Enthusiast: Used Books

If you are content starting as a smaller, hobby-type store, you will want to start by collecting your first sale items from books you already have on hand. You may also find these at garage sales, antique shops, and estate sales on the occasional weekend shopping trip.

This type of shop is a great way to begin a Business. You would do well to start your business as a shop on Amazon that's dedicated to books. You can create social media accounts for this shop and use it as your storefront.

Book Aficionado: Used and New Books

If you are ready to plunge into online bookstore ownership with both feet, it's important you consider the ability to have many copies of books on hand. You can sell both used and new books, but if you choose to sell new, you will need to search for book suppliers with good prices that can afford you a sufficient markup. The challenge here is comparing your prices with popular online stores like Amazon. If you can't beat Amazon's prices, you'll have a hard time selling your books.

This selling opportunity also opens you up for a more serious approach to selling rare and used books in great condition. This type of used book selling will require a lot of research to accurately price rare books as well as to correctly describe them and make them as discoverable online as possible in order to attract customers who will pay your prices.

This type of store may require more research before starting, but is the perfect opportunity for someone who enjoys rare books and research involving books.

When considering opening an online bookstore, ask yourself what type of store you want to open and what your platform will be. Some options to specify are:

- Offering only rare books
- Genre specific stores
- New releases only
- Local books
- Little known authors

You don't necessarily have to narrow it down, but it can help you create a specific draw to your store. If you hone your focus (and maybe that's only at the beginning) you can become a type of "authority" on the specific line of books you sell, making your store that much more valuable.

Step by Step: What you'll need to sell books online

These steps may vary depending on the type of store you wish to start, but they hold principles that are true for both kinds of stores.

1. Collect your books and do your research

After you've decided what type of store you will open, set up your storage space (with consideration to temperature and humidity of the space) and start collecting books. This time will also be important to do research for any rare books you will want to sell. The more effort you put into organization before hand, the less you will have to worry about after your store opens.

2. Open for business

When you have completed your research and collected stock for your store, setup your online storefront. Whether that's on Amazon or a website that allows you to sell items, make your space as inviting and understandable as possible. Make sure you keep things updated in a timely manner with an eye toward establishing a strong online presence with excellent customer service.

3. Spread the word

Marketing will play a large role in this portion of your business setup. Let your friends, family, and extended network know that you've opened a store. It is a good idea to share with local reading groups, online groups (think of finding groups on Goodreads), and even seeking out associations you can join to further the spread of your stores name.

4. **Be on the lookout**

Once you've completed these steps and opened for business, it will then be part of your job description to always be on the lookout. You may spend weekends at antique or estate sales or you may go garage sale hunting on a regular basis, but you will always want to be adding stock to your store.

If you are selling new books, find great printer and/or publishers to strike up deals with in order to sell their books. This will mean that you need to keep an eye toward the trends in the market and new releases coming out.

Spend Less

To spend less when starting up your online bookstore, the furthest you have to go is to your own bookshelves.

- Start up a used bookstore on Amazon with books you have on hand
- Sell when it is convenient (and when you have stock)
- Only purchase (and sell) used books
- Find "free book" tables at bookstores or at library events to find free books that you can resell
- Branch out and include other media items like used CDs or DVDs

Spend More

If you have a larger budget to work with, we recommend:

- Purchase rare used books to resell (these will cost more and you must be able to guarantee that you will get a good return on your investment)
- Establish a good relationship with a publisher and purchase regularly from them in order to provide consistent, new titles to your customers
- Purchase a brick and mortar store: Should your online store do extremely well, why not open an actual store?

Chapter 6

Writing Business: Write Your Way Into A Career

Once you understand how the freelance writing business works and have a brand built up, you can outsource the work, start your own blog, and sell affiliate products through an email list. When it comes to the content business sky is the limit.

You can start as a freelance writer or a blogger and work your way up. Do you have the gift of words? Do English rules, grammar, and the *Chicago Manual of Style* send tingles up your arms? If so, a job as a freelance writer is the perfect job for you to start with!

The Benefits

- Simple Setup

There are almost no costs associated with becoming a freelance writer. Once you have a computer and Internet connection to work from, you can begin writing for a client within days.

- Easy to Scale-up

Once you understand how the freelance writing business works and have a brand built up, you can outsource the work, start your own blog, and sell affiliate products. Sky is the limit

- Flexible Hours

Freelancers have flexible hours. These hours are determined by the project of the client you are working for and their personal due date. You can have the luxury of working in the mornings or the evenings; the key is getting your work done well and on time.

- Many Areas of Need

The beauty of starting a freelance writing career is the fact that there are many areas of need for content, editing, and creation. You can focus on one area of writing or take on multiple tasks, depending on your available time and abilities.

The Drawbacks

- Establish Credibility

When considering a small business as a freelancer you are limited by your own knowledge. Having a solid grasp of English and rules of grammar is essential, though a degree is not always necessary.

- Time

Freelancing does take up time. This will depend on the project, but you are most limited by the number of words you can type per minute and the research required for any writing you may do. Also, many projects will be time-based and you will need to accomplish them quickly and accurately.

- Payment

This drawback is slightly conditional. Many freelance writers will find that they must begin their business at a lower rate of return for the work that they do in order to find clients. For beginning freelancers, you can expect to receive below .01 cents per word. As your reputation and experience grows, you will be able to raise your prices and have the freedom to choose your clients. This is a drawback due to the fact that, in order to build your portfolio, you will likely have to work for less than you may deserve at first.

- Fees

If you use an online platform to help kick start your business, you will find that these platforms take a fee from the payment you receive. It is best to include these fees in your prices whenever possible.

What you need

- A computer
- Internet Connection
- Inspiration

*This may be the shortest list of "needs" we've created, but it's true. There isn't much more you will need.

Step by Step: What it takes to become a freelance writer

1. Make a Decision

The first step to becoming a freelance writer is to make a decision about what type of freelance writing you will pursue. There are many types and areas where you can explore freelance writing.

- Content and Copywriting
- Article writing
- Blogging
- Product descriptions
- Product reviews
- Editing (posts, articles, books)
- eBook writing (fiction and non-fiction)
- Manuscript or idea critique

- Plot outlining
- Professional and Academic writing
- Ghost writing

In some cases you may combine many of these into a package to offer clients or to diversify in order to have a full client list.

2. Create a portfolio

The next step to starting your freelance business is to compile (or create) a portfolio to showcase your writing ability. In some cases this may require that you create examples of your work, in other cases you may be able to use things you've already written. Either way, we recommend you create PDF copies of examples of what you will offer your clients.

This will also be a good time to compile reviews from anyone you've worked with before and previous publications of your work. A list of credentials will also be helpful to list in order to create the most credible profile possible.

3. Get Online

There are many ways to start a freelance business online. We'll take a look at two here:

- Personal Website

First, you can start your own personal website (or even a blog with a customized domain name) where you offer your services. The difficulty of this is approach is gaining a steady flow of clients. This option may be best left for later in your career when you are established as a freelance writer with experience behind you.

- Online Platform

There are many online platforms (like Elance, oDesk, Freelancer, and Fiverr to name a few) that offer a great way to start up a freelance business. The downside to these sites are the fees they charge, but when you are starting your business, you will find that they are very helpful platforms to facilitate writer/client interaction.

4. **Write away**

After you have established yourself on an online platform or personal webpage, you will find opportunities to work for clients. In some cases you will need to send proposals outlining your previous experience (which is where #1 and #2 will come in handy) and at times clients will come to you. Keep an eye toward detail, work quality, customer service, and a quick turnaround time.

Spend Less

With regards to starting up a freelancing career you don't need to spend much money. Some freelance sites may require a monthly fee for you to join, but many are free. The only money spent is the initial cost of a computer to begin your freelance business.

Spend More

Should you come to a point in your freelance career where you are willing to invest more money, one area of investment is additional education. There may be an area of writing that you'd like to move into. This is a great opportunity to invest in classes and online certifications that will land you higher paying clients in the future. You can also spend additional funds on marketing your skills and creating a top-notch website.

Chapter 7

Independent Consulting: How To Sell What You Know

In the market of small business today, there is a growing need for knowledge. As you were brainstorming, you came up with things you were passionate about, ideas you have, and talents that go alongside these things. Now it's time to take out those dreams and put feet to them.

What can you do, or teach others to do, that you can *market*?

It may seem like a strange concept, but there is a high price for knowledge on the market and, with the proper setup and marketing strategy, you could find yourself coaching, advising, or giving input for a living. Often we immediately think of financial or tax consultants, but we can broaden this idea to leadership coaching, social media and marketing consultants, graphic design consultants, and business advisors. There are so many more positions available though. You are only limited in the amount of time, resources, and energy you can give toward this position.

The Benefits

- You're the boss

Being a consultant can take many different forms, but the fact of the matter is: you're the boss. You will be in charge of your marketing plan (even if you hire this out to someone else) and you will create your workspace – whether that is at a coffee shop down the street from your home or in Paris, France for the week. All you need is an Internet connection.

- Specialize

Another benefit to being an independent consultant is that you can choose the area you will specialize in. This will play to *your* strengths and will mean that you are working in your highest capacity at all times.

- Endless Possibilities

There really are endless possibilities for independent coaching and advising. You will be able to decide what you can offer based on your talents and what you have built a reputation for.

The Drawbacks

- Certificates

For some positions, especially in the financial sector, you will be required to have certificates. This isn't necessarily a drawback, but it could put your dream job on hold until you can get the certificates in place.

- Credibility

People consult with someone for coaching and expert advice because they *are* that, an expert. You must be able to prove that you have the credentials to provide the service you say you will. If you offer financial advice, you will likely need to have proof of previous work experience, just as you would need experience in marketing, writing, or graphic design. Treat this just as you would any other job and create a type of "resume" for potential clients to see.

It is good to note that a strong, online presence will do wonders for your consulting business. Spend your time wisely by building up a fan base that comes to you for your knowledge so that, when you offer your services, people are willing to pay for your expert advice.

Step by Step: What it takes to be an independent consultant

The steps to independent consulting will look differently depending on the industry you choose. If it is part of the business realm, you will want to have established credentials and any certificates you will need. If you are planning on working in a more creative type of coaching, then you will need a portfolio to show your clients. Even fitness coaching is a lucrative idea that can easily be started at home.

In some cases this may mean working for free or minimal payment until you have sufficiently built up your portfolio. It may seem like wasted time, but it isn't. It is the best way to establish credibility while in the beginning stages of your business.

We recommend these steps:

1. Establish your idea

This is the most crucial step. Just as it's important to establish your brand when beginning *any* business, you must establish you idea and brand before you do anything else.

This should include:

- Your main idea and purpose statement
- You business plan with short-term and long-term goals
- The services you will provide and their prices
- Marketing strategy
- A potential clientele list you could essentially "cold call"

When starting up a business it's a great idea to offer your services at a reduced rate to attract clients. Only work for free in the startup phase. When it's time to charge for your services, offer a friend and family discount. This lets your clients know that they won't always be able to take advantage of your services at such a reduced rate.

2. Setup your website

This is the second most important part of your setup process. Your website will be your hub for all things business-related. Choose a platform that allows you to setup a commerce section to accept payments as well as one that has all of the functionality that you need. In line with this, purchase your domain name as well. This will ensure you can attract traffic to your site easily. It also will give a professional appearance to your business.

Don't forget:

- Professional Marketing Materials: Including a logo, business cards, printed materials, and graphics (these can be purchased at reduced rates without completely sacrificing quality).
- Professional headshots: Do not use a selfie or low quality photo. This will undermine your professional appearance.
- Online payment system: Think PayPal or Square. It must be something that will allow you to take payments easily. (You will want to anticipate their fees and incorporate them in your overall price).

3. Market Assessment

Take an opportunity to do an assessment of your market. Who are you competing with? What do they offer their clients? What are their clients saying about their services? This is not to copy what they do, but to assess what you are offering. If you have packages that offer service fees significantly higher than your competition, you may not receive as much business if you were to lower them (for a time).

Take regular assessments of your current market and always be on the lookout for ways to engage those from other areas.

4. Get Reviews

Word of mouth is one of the absolute *best* ways to attract customers. If you have decided to offer your services at a reduced rate to friends and family, ask them for reviews (make sure to ask for permission to post them). The more reviews you get the better word of your services will travel.

Use these reviews on your marketing material and in your social media posting.

5. Keep going

This last point is obvious, but often times overlooked. When starting a small business it is common to be blinded by excitement. When reality hits and you haven't attracted as many clients as you'd initially hoped for, it is easy to despair. Don't!

Tenacity will win out in the end. The best advice we can give you is to *keep going*. This means consistent posting on your blog and social media, reaching out to new areas and markets, asking more friends for reviews in exchange for services, or even asking professionals in similar markets for advice. Either way, it often can take up to three years for you to start to feel truly successful. This isn't always the case, but we encourage you to be prepared to put in hard work in order to receive those amazing benefits.

What You Need

This is a list of things it will be helpful to have to start an independent consulting venture:

- Computer
- Certifications and/or past client experience
- Website and blog
- Marketing materials (business cards, mailers, brochures)
- Online advertisements

Spend Less

When beginning an independent consulting Business, there are many areas you could spend money. Here are some ideas on how to save:

- Use an armature photographer for your headshots (A note of caution here, look at his or her work beforehand to make sure they will provide a level of quality that is acceptable).
- Trade your services for products or advice you may need to get your business up and running.
- Network among your own friends. It's always best to start by sharing what you're doing as something you are passionate about, not necessarily for a sale. You never know what connections you could make.

- Share, share, and share on social media! Build your audience even before you start offering your services.
- Work part-time. This may cut into your dedicated time, but if you are struggling to make it solely on a new consulting business, you may need to supplement until you can afford to devote all of your time to your new business.

Spend More

Should you have additional capital to spend on your consulting venture, we recommend spending in these areas:

- Effective, targeted marketing: This may mean hiring someone to help you or spending money on certain ads, either way be sure to track your success/loss with every advertisement.
- High quality materials. Never underestimate the power of a great quality business card.
- Consider shooting a video. Options for video can range in price, but they are a great way for your potential clients to hear from you before they even decided to hire you.
- Purchase (better) tools of the trade (this will depend on what type of consulting you venture into).
- Raise your prices. While this doesn't fit the "spend more" category exactly, it does fall in line with a decision you will make when business is better. When you notice your time is becoming overly full, weed out some of the lower paying clients by raising your prices to work on less projects but for the same (or increased) rate.

Chapter 8

Should I Quit My Job?

Now the topic you have been waiting for, unless you skipped straight to it of course! When should you quit your full time job to work on your business full time?

This is a personal question and is usually best answered by taking a look at your finances and deciding how your time and money can best suit you. There is also something to be said about taking a "leap of faith" as well.

If you truly believe in yourself and that you will be successful in your business than by all means quit your job and go after your dreams. There is also nothing wrong with staying at your job and launching your business slowly over time.

Review the section where I talk about making money fast and see if any of those ideas sound appealing to you. You might be able to make enough money with one of those strategies than you can afford to quit your job so that you can spend majority of your time on your business.

The one thing you have to really think about is what will work best for you. Some people can work a full time job and launch a business. Some people may need to just focus 100% on the business to be able to make it successful. Figure out which type of person you are and then go with it.

You will know when it's time to quit. You might be scared to do it but you'll have that nagging feeling that just won't go away. That is the sign that you are ready.

It is also important to realize that quitting your job to start a business is a risk. Some risks pay off and some do not. You have to be willing to accept that. Your original business idea might turn out to be a dud. You may have to change course on the fly and try a different one. This is normal.

Most successful business owners faced a lot of setbacks before they succeeded. If early on you struggle just remember that. Once you do finally quit your job you will be filled with excitement but as soon as that first setback comes you will be second guessing your decision. Stay positive and keep pushing, this is normal. Just keep making progress and do not quit! You will eventually succeed.

Another thing is that a lot of people will probably think you are crazy for quitting your job to start a business. You have to be willing to accept that too.

They will also try to give you all kinds of advice on how to do things. Only listen to people who you feel are truly qualified to give you advice, meaning they are someone who has actually done what they are talking about. If you try to listen to everyone else you will end up getting nowhere.

One last point about quitting your job, don't burn bridges. If you are leaving your company, try to leave on good terms and give proper notice. Some of the people you previously worked with could become your future customers.

You could also end up doing business with your previous employer. You never really know what can happen in the future, it is always better to leave everything on better terms than started!

Long Term Vision

Now let's talk about your long term vision for your business. This is the vision that you had all along of where you would eventually like to take your business. We're not just thinking quick cash and in the short term here.

What are you going to need to reach your goals and get your business to where you would like it to be? Do you need a web site? Social media profiles? Do you need an office? Will you need outside help?

These are all questions that you should be asking yourself as you grow your business and strive towards reaching your ultimate vision. If your plan is to get BIG, you may want to start looking into investors to pitch in or a crowd source funding to get things underway. It is also time to look realistically at where you see your business in 5 - 10 years.

Make sure that you keep things simple at first; you do not want to add complication to the mix until you are firmly established. You don't have to reach your ultimate vision of your business anytime soon. You just want to make sure you know the directions you want to head and take baby steps towards it.

Make sure you listen to your customers too. They will be the ones who will show you potential problems that you didn't even know existed. This feedback is extremely valuable and will aid you in reaching your long term goals.

Believe In Yourself!

The most important part of quitting your job and starting a business of your own is belief in yourself! You can have everything else figure out but if you don't truly believe that you can actually make this happen, you won't. If you believe in yourself, you will eventually be successful. There is no doubt about it.

Belief is what is going to get you through working the long hours and doing the dirty work to get your business up and running. Negative thinking can ruin your business before you even start it. I'd definitely recommend making sure your mindset is right before deciding to embark on this journey. It is normal to have some doubts but if you are outright telling yourself "I can't do this", then you won't. You are what you think, as simple as that may sound it is the truth.

You also have to have passion for what you do. If you don't then you will not have the motivation to see it through. Being your own boss and starting your own business sounds great, but make sure that you are doing something you truly love and care about. If you don't have passion for what you are doing it will be difficult to make it through all the struggles and all the hard work that starting a successful business requires.

In the end you will find that being your own boss is infinitely more enjoyable than any job someone else can provide. There is never an ideal time to start your own business.

The best time to do it is now, while you are still young, while you are still full of life! You don't want to be old and on your death bed with regrets! The satisfaction you will get from actually doing it is something you will never regret. It is an amazing feeling to be able to provide tangible value to the world. So quit reading and get started! Today is the day you go out and get started on your business!